LOVING THE LORD

Daily Pursuits of a Love That Never Fails

A 31-Day Devotional

Dr. John Aniemeke

LOVING THE LORD

Copyright ©2025 **John Aniemeke**

Paperback ISBN: 978-1-965593-73-8

All rights reserved. No part of this publication may be reproduced, distributed, or transmitted in any form or by any means, including photocopying, recording, or other electronic or mechanical methods, without the prior written permission of the author except in the case of brief quotations embodied in reviews and certain other non-commercial uses permitted by copyright law. Otherwise stated Scripture quotations designated NIV are taken from the New International Version.

All rights reserved.

Published by Cornerstone Publishing

A Division of Cornerstone Creativity Group LLC
Info@thecornerstonepublishers.com
www.thecornerstonepublishers.com

Author's Contact

To book the author to speak at your next event or to order bulk copies of this book, please, use this email:

janiemeke@yahoo.com

Printed in the United States of America.

CONTENTS

Introduction 5
1. Created for His Glory and Love 8
2. God Loved Us First 10
3. Loving God with All Our Heart 12
4. Loving God with All Our Soul 14
5. Loving God with All Our Minds 16
6. Loving God with All Our Strength 18
7. Loving God by Loving Others 20
8. Setting the Lord as Our Focus 22
9. Delighting in the Lord 24
10. Talking About His Faithfulness 26
11. Loving Him in Praise and Worship 29
12. Dwelling in His House 31
13. Obedience as the Greatest Expression of Love 33
14. Guarding Our Love Against Worldliness 35
15. Loving Others as Ourselves 37
16. Encouraging Our Household to Love the Lord 39
17. Generous and Sacrificial Giving 41
18. Feeding His Sheep 44
19. Passion for Souls and Evangelism 46

20. Zeal for God's House..................................49
21. Loving God in the Midst of Trials......................51
22. Intimacy with God.....................................53
23. Access to God's Best..................................55
24. Covenant Blessings for Those Who Love Him.....57
25. Faithfulness and Divine Acknowledgment...........59
26. All Things Work Together for Lovers of God.....61
27. Divine Rescue and Protection..........................63
28. Peace and Contentment................................65
29. Transformation and Spiritual Growth................67
30. Purpose and Fulfillment...............................71
31. Loving God: The Key to Eternal Life................73

One-Year Bible Reading Plan..............................75

INTRODUCTION

Loving the Lord is the highest calling of every believer. Jesus said that the greatest commandment is to *"love the Lord your God with all your heart and with all your soul and with all your mind and with all your strength"* (Mark 12:30). Everything in our Christian walk flows from this truth. When our love for God is alive and growing, our faith deepens, our purpose becomes clear, and our lives overflow with His presence.

This 31-day devotional is designed to help you cultivate that love in a practical and intentional way. Each day provides:

- A **Scripture reading** to anchor your heart in God's Word.

- A **reflection** with stories and illustrations to make the truth relatable and real.

- A **closing prayer** to guide your conversation with God.

- **Prayer points** that help you press deeper into the theme and personalize it for your own life.

Here are a few suggestions as you begin this journey:

- **Set aside a daily time with God.** Choose a consistent moment — morning, evening, or even during your lunch break — to sit with the Lord through this devotional. Treat it as a sacred appointment.

- **Read slowly and reflect.** Don't rush through the Scriptures or reflections. Pause and ask yourself, *"How does this apply to my life today?"*

- **Pray with intention.** Use the prayer points to go deeper. Pray them out loud, personalize them, and let them lead you into heartfelt conversation with God.

- **Write it down.** Keep a journal of what God speaks to you each day. Over 31 days, you will see how His Spirit is shaping and transforming your heart.

- **Share the journey.** This devotional can be used personally, with family, or in small groups. Reading together, discussing insights, and praying the points aloud with others can spark fresh fire of revival and renewal in the community.

Most importantly, don't view this devotional as another task to complete, but as an invitation into a deeper relationship. Even if you miss a day, simply pick back up — God is more interested in your heart than your checklist.

As you walk through these pages, may your love for the Lord grow richer and stronger. May you discover joy in His presence, peace in His promises, and purpose in His plan for your life. And may this 31-day journey ignite a passion for God that continues long after the final page.

Day 1

CREATED FOR HIS GLORY AND LOVE

Scripture:

Luke 10:27 – *"Love the Lord your God with all your heart and with all your soul and with all your strength and with all your mind."*

Isaiah 43:7 – *"Everyone who is called by my name, whom I created for my glory, whom I formed and made."*

Reflection:

You were not created by accident. You were created for a singular purpose of loving God and reflecting His glory. He formed us for Himself and for His pleasure (Revelation 4:11). At the very center of your existence is this truth: your life finds meaning when it is rooted in loving the Lord.

When expectant parents prepare for a child, they paint the nursery, fold tiny clothes, and dream of the future. Every detail is marked by love and intention. You were fearfully and wonderfully created to show forth His praises (Psalm 139:14). In a greater way, God fashioned you with purpose. Your existence is not random. You were made to know Him, to love Him, and to carry His glory wherever you go.

David understood this when he declared, *"Because Your lovingkindness is better than life, my lips shall praise You"* (Psalm 63:3). Life without loving God becomes empty no matter how successful it may look. But when we live out our love for Him, even ordinary days become filled with joy, peace, and purpose.

The first step in this devotional journey is to recognize that loving God is not an option or an extra; it is your primary assignment in life. You were created for His glory, and loving Him is the way you fulfill that purpose.

Closing Prayer:

Father, thank You for creating me with purpose and love. I choose today to live for Your glory. Teach me to love You above all else and let my life reflect Your beauty. In Jesus' name, Amen.

Prayer Points:

- Lord, help me to live daily with the awareness that I was created for Your glory.

- Father, let my love for You grow stronger than my love for anything else in this world.

- Holy Spirit, align my thoughts, desires, and actions with God's purpose for my life.

Day 2

GOD LOVED US FIRST

Scripture:

1 John 4:10 – *"This is love: not that we loved God, but that He loved us and sent His Son as an atoning sacrifice for our sins."*

1 John 4:19 – *"We love because He first loved us."*

Reflection:

Our love for God doesn't start with us; it starts with Him. Long before you even thought about praying, worshiping, or following Jesus, God had already chosen to love you. He loved you first. Apart from His enabling grace, we are incapable of loving Him rightly. It is God who works within us, both to will and to act according to His good pleasure (Philippians 2:13).

A child learning to walk. They take wobbly steps and often fall, but the parents' arms are already reaching out to catch them. That's how God feels about us. His love is there, ready to embrace us, even before we take a step toward Him. Long before any prayer crossed your lips, He had already made the first move through Christ.

Sometimes, we find it hard to feel worthy of God's love because of our failures or shortcomings. But His love isn't dependent on how well we perform; it's rooted in who He is. The cross stands as the ultimate proof of this — He gave everything before we had a chance to give anything back.

When you truly grasp this, your love for God transforms into a joyful response rather than a heavy burden. You don't love Him to earn His favor; you love Him because you already have it.

Closing Prayer:

Father, thank You for loving me first. Your love is undeserved, unchanging, and unconditional. Help me to live each day in gratitude to Your amazing love. In Jesus' name, Amen.

Prayer Points:

- Lord, open my heart to fully understand and embrace Your love for me.
- Thank You, Father, for sending Jesus as the proof of Your love; help me never to take it for granted.
- Holy Spirit, let my love for God overflow into my relationships and actions.

Day 3

LOVING GOD WITH ALL OUR HEART

Scripture:

Deuteronomy 6:5 – *"Love the Lord your God with all your heart and with all your soul and with all your strength."*

Reflection:

The heart is truly the center of our emotions and desires. To love God with all our heart means giving Him our deepest affections and placing Him above every other love in our lives.

In the early days of marriage, couples often invest a lot of energy into surprises, long conversations, and small gestures that show their devotion. However, as time goes on, it takes intentional effort to keep that flame alive. Our relationship with God is no different — our love for Him flourishes when we nurture it daily, rather than leaving it to chance.

Jesus warned in Matthew 24:12 that *"the love of many will grow cold."* Life's distractions, disappointments, and temptations can easily choke our devotion. Yet, when we keep our hearts focused on Him, we discover renewed joy and passion. Like David, we can proclaim, *"I will praise You, O Lord my God, with all my heart; I will glorify Your name* forevermore" (Psalm 86:12).

If I were to audit my heart today, what would its affections reveal? Would they point toward God, or toward other competing desires? If our affections tilt away from Him, then realignment is necessary. Everything we become flows from what our hearts cherish most.

Loving God with all your heart isn't about a half-hearted Sunday routine; it's about making Him the center of your affections every single day.

Closing Prayer:

Lord, I give You my whole heart today. Let my love for You be undivided and sincere. Guard my heart from distractions and fill it with a passion for Your presence. In Jesus' name, Amen.

Prayer Points:

- Father, purify my heart from every competing love that draws me away from You.

- Lord, ignite in me a fresh fire of devotion that will never grow cold.

- Holy Spirit, help me to love God with sincerity, faithfulness, and joy.

Day 4

LOVING GOD WITH ALL OUR SOUL

Scripture:

Matthew 22:37 – *"Jesus replied: 'Love the Lord your God with all your heart and with all your soul and with all your mind.'"*

Reflection:

The soul is where our emotions, will, and personality reside. To love God with all your soul means to align your very identity with Him. It's not just about what you do, but about who you are.

Musicians often lose themselves in their music. The sounds they create are more than just skill; they reflect who they are at their core. Loving God with your soul is similar. It's not about performance; it's about identity. It's not a role you play, but the essence of who you are.

Naomi, in the book of Ruth, felt her life was over when she returned to Bethlehem feeling empty and bitter. However, when Ruth clung to her, declaring,

"Your people will be my people, and your God my God" (Ruth 1:16), we witness a profound commitment. Ruth wasn't just following Naomi; she was tying her life to the God of Israel. That's what it means to love God with your soul — it's a love that connects your entire identity to Him.

When storms arise, loving God with your soul keeps you grounded. It means that no matter what changes around you, your innermost being remains anchored in Him.

Closing Prayer:

Lord, I surrender my soul, my thoughts, emotions, and will to You. Shape my identity and desires so they reflect my love for You. In Jesus' name, Amen.

Prayer Points:

- Father, let my soul find its rest and satisfaction in You alone.
- Lord, heal every broken area of my soul and align it with Your will.
- Holy Spirit, help me to express my love for God through the choices I make each day.

Day 5

LOVING GOD WITH ALL OUR MINDS

Scripture:

Romans 12:2 – *"Do not conform to the pattern of this world, but be transformed by the renewing of your mind. Then you will be able to test and approve what God's will is — His good, pleasing and perfect will."*

Reflection:

To love God with all your mind means surrendering your thoughts, reasoning, and imagination to Him. Our minds are powerful; they shape our choices, habits, and ultimately, our destiny. This is why the enemy constantly battles for our thoughts.

Think of a gardener tending to a field. If weeds are left unchecked, they can overrun the good plants. Similarly, when we allow negative, sinful, or worldly thoughts to linger, they choke out our devotion to God. But when we nurture our minds with the Word of God, we start to think His thoughts, dream His dreams, and see life through His eyes.

Daniel serves as a clear example of this. As a young

man in Babylon, he was surrounded by a culture that sought to reshape his identity and thinking. Yet he made a firm decision in his mind not to defile himself (Daniel 1:8). His devotion to God was evident not only in his heart but also in his mind. That choice shaped his entire life and legacy.

To love God with your mind means allowing His Word to renew your thinking each day. It involves replacing lies with truth, fear with faith, and confusion with clarity.

It's important to fix our minds on every attribute that constitutes loving the Lord (Philippians 4:8).

Closing Prayer:

Father, I dedicate my mind to You today. Fill it with Your wisdom, cleanse it from every lie, and let my thoughts align with Your truth. In Jesus' name, Amen.

Prayer Points:

- Lord, renew my mind daily through Your Word and guard my thoughts from the enemy's lies.

- Father, give me the mind of Christ so I can discern Your will in every situation.

- Holy Spirit, train my thoughts to dwell on what is true, noble, pure, and praiseworthy (Philippians 4:8).

Day 6

LOVING GOD WITH ALL OUR STRENGTH

Scripture:

Mark 12:30 – *"Love the Lord your God with all your heart and with all your soul and with all your mind and with all your strength."*

Reflection:

Strength embodies energy, effort, and resources. To love God with all your strength means offering Him your best in action—not just through words or emotions, but through your daily choices, habits, and work.

Athletes invest their energy into training, discipline their bodies, and push past limits because they see the prize ahead. That same determination is what loving God with our strength looks like. It's not merely expressing devotion but giving Him the best of our time, energy, and effort as an act of love.

The Apostle Paul wrote, *"I will very gladly spend and be spent for your souls"* (2 Corinthians 12:15). His love for

God overflowed into sacrificial service, even when it cost him comfort, reputation, and safety.

Sometimes we say, "I love God," but we only give Him what's left after work, hobbies, or personal interests. Loving God with our strength means rearranging our priorities to ensure He receives the first and best of our efforts. It's not about working for His love but working *from* His love. Ask yourself today: Am I giving God my best, or just what's convenient?

Closing Prayer:

Lord, I give You my strength. Use my energy, time, and resources for Your glory. Teach me to serve You with joy and excellence in everything I do. In Jesus' name, Amen.

Prayer Points:

- Father, strengthen me daily to love and serve You wholeheartedly.
- Lord, help me to use my gifts, time, and resources as an offering of love to You.
- Holy Spirit, empower me to remain faithful and diligent in serving God, even when it requires sacrifice.

Day 7

LOVING GOD BY LOVING OTHERS

Scripture:

Luke 10:25–27 – *"Love the Lord your God with all your heart and with all your soul and with all your strength and with all your mind; and, 'Love your neighbor as yourself.'"*

John 13:35 – *"By this everyone will know that you are my disciples, if you love one another."*

Reflection:

Our love for God is most clearly shown in how we treat others. Jesus connected these two commandments — to love God and to love our neighbor. You can't truly say you love God if you harbor disdain for the people He created.

On a dusty road between Jerusalem and Jericho, a wounded man lay helpless while others walked by. It was a Samaritan, seen as an outsider, who stopped to help him. That simple act of kindness revealed more about love for God than any ritual or title ever could. Genuine devotion is always visible in the way we treat those around us.

When we truly love God, it naturally spills over into compassion for others. It's evident in our patience with a challenging coworker, our kindness toward a neighbor, or our generosity to someone in need. Sometimes, the most powerful sermon you can deliver isn't from a pulpit, but through a simple act of love.

The Apostle John wrote, *"If anyone says, 'I love God,' but hates his brother, he is a liar"* (1 John 4:20). Our love for others serves as the true evidence of our love for God. Do we love our neighbor, the stranger, and the co-worker as an outflow of our love for God? Or do we practice selective love? True love is unconditional.

Closing Prayer:

Lord, help me to love others the way You have loved me. Teach me to show kindness, patience, and compassion, even when it's hard. Let my love for people be a reflection of my love for You. In Jesus' name, Amen.

Prayer Points:

- Father, fill my heart with compassion for people, so that I may love them as You do.
- Lord, help me to forgive and show grace to those who hurt me.
- Holy Spirit, make me a channel of God's love in my family, workplace, and community.

Day 8

SETTING THE LORD AS OUR FOCUS

Scripture:

Psalm 16:8 – *"I have set the LORD always before me: because He is at my right hand, I shall not be moved."*

Deuteronomy 4:29 – *"But if from there you seek the LORD your God, you will find Him if you seek Him with all your heart and with all your soul."*

Reflection:

Loving God starts with focus. What we concentrate on grows stronger in our lives. To keep the Lord at the forefront means making Him central to our attention, choices, and desires.

Imagine a driver fixated on the rearview mirror instead of the road ahead—it's easy to see how they'd drift off course. Focus shapes our direction. Similarly, when distractions or fears take over our attention, we stumble. But when Christ is our focal point, our steps remain steady, regardless of how fierce the storm may be.

Peter experienced this firsthand when he stepped out of the boat to walk on water (Matthew 14:29–30). As long as he kept his eyes on Jesus, he walked triumphantly over the waves. However, when he shifted his focus to the wind and storm, he began to sink. This principle holds true for us today: our focus influences our faith.

Making the Lord a priority isn't a one-time choice; it's a daily commitment. It involves starting each day with prayer, immersing ourselves in His Word, and inviting Him into every decision. When God becomes your focus, everything else falls into place.

Closing Prayer:

Lord, I choose today to set You always before me. Help me fix my eyes on You and not be distracted by the storms around me. Keep me steady in Your love. In Jesus' name, Amen.

Prayer Points:

- Father, teach me to keep my eyes fixed on You in every season of life.

- Lord, deliver me from distractions that pull me away from Your presence.

- Holy Spirit, help me develop daily habits that keep God at the center of my focus.

Day 9

DELIGHTING IN THE LORD

Scripture:

Psalm 37:4 – *"Delight yourself also in the LORD, and He shall give you the desires of your heart."*

Isaiah 58:14 – *"Then you will find your joy in the LORD, and I will cause you to ride in triumph on the heights of the land."*

Reflection:

To delight in the Lord is to find joy, pleasure, and satisfaction in Him. It's about choosing God not out of obligation but out of genuine delight. When you truly enjoy being in His presence, obedience flows naturally, and worship becomes a joyful experience.

A skilled musician knows that an instrument must be carefully tuned before it can produce beautiful music. Even a slight misalignment causes every note to sound off, no matter how talented the player may be. In the same way, when our hearts are tuned to God, our lives produce harmony. But when distractions pull us out of alignment, everything begins to feel strained and unsettled. Delighting in the Lord keeps our hearts properly tuned to His presence.

David captured this in Psalm 27:4 when he wrote, *"One thing I ask from the LORD, this only do I seek: that I may dwell in the house of the LORD all the days of my life, to gaze on the beauty of the LORD and to seek Him in His temple."* For David, delighting in God was not just an extra activity — it was his deepest desire.

When we delight in the Lord, He aligns our desires with His will. The promise of Psalm 37:4 is not that God gives us everything we want, but that He reshapes our desires so they align with His perfect plan.

Without Him, we amount to nothing. As this truth takes root, God becomes our supreme delight, and we experience an unexplainable joy that draws us repeatedly into fellowship with Him.

Closing Prayer:

Father, let my greatest joy be found in You. Teach me to delight in Your presence more than in any temporary pleasure this world offers. In Jesus' name, Amen.

Prayer Points:

- Lord, give me a heart that finds joy in Your presence daily.
- Father, align my desires with Your will as I delight in You.
- Holy Spirit, help me to see the beauty of God in every season of life.

Day 10

TALKING ABOUT HIS FAITHFULNESS

Scripture:

Isaiah 63:7 – *"I will tell of the kindnesses of the LORD, the deeds for which He is to be praised, according to all the LORD has done for us — yes, the many good things He has done for Israel, according to His compassion and many kindnesses."*

Psalm 71:15 – *"My mouth will tell of Your righteous acts, of Your deeds of salvation all day long — though their number is past my knowledge."*

Reflection:

One of the most powerful ways to express our love for God is by sharing stories of His faithfulness. Every testimony you share is an act of love and respect toward Him, showing the world that He is trustworthy and good.

We naturally talk about what excites us — whether it's a new restaurant, a great book, or a touching story. Gratitude has a way of finding its voice, and it spreads easily. Similarly, when we share our experiences of

God's faithfulness, our words become a testimony that honors Him and inspires faith in those who listen. Silence may withhold glory, but sharing our testimonies multiplies it.

In the Old Testament, the Israelites were often reminded to remember and tell of God's works. When they forgot, their faith weakened. But when they shared their experiences, their love for God grew stronger. The same holds true today. Your story of answered prayer, healing, or provision can uplift someone else and encourage them to trust Him.

Talking about God's faithfulness isn't limited to church services; it's meant for everyday life. In your family, workplace, or community, you can show others that your God is alive and active. Sharing your testimony not only strengthens faith but also honors God and keeps your love for Him alive.

Closing Prayer:

Lord, I will never stop speaking of Your goodness. Let my mouth declare Your faithfulness and inspire others to trust in You. In Jesus' name, Amen.

Prayer Points:

- Father, remind me daily of Your goodness so I never take it for granted.

- Lord, give me boldness to share testimonies of Your faithfulness with others.

- Holy Spirit, use my words to point people to God's love and power.

Day 11

LOVING HIM IN PRAISE AND WORSHIP

Scripture:

Psalm 103:1–2 – *"Bless the LORD, O my soul; and all that is within me, bless His holy name. Bless the LORD, O my soul, and forget not all His benefits."*

John 4:23 – *"But the hour is coming, and is now here, when the true worshipers will worship the Father in spirit and truth, for the Father is seeking such people to worship Him."*

Reflection:

Praise and worship are more than just songs; they are heartfelt expressions of love for God. When you worship, you convey to God that He is worthy of your affection, attention, and devotion.

When friends come together to celebrate a birthday, the songs, words, and laughter reflect the value of the occasion. Worship does something similar, but on a much deeper level. It goes beyond music or routine — it's the language of love poured out to God, affirming His worth no matter what season we find ourselves in.

Paul and Silas truly understood this when they were imprisoned (Acts 16:25). At midnight, they prayed and sang hymns to God. Their worship wasn't influenced by their circumstances; it was simply an overflow of love. And in response, God sent an earthquake that broke their chains.

True worship comes from the heart. It isn't about musical style or church tradition; it's about a sincere response of love. When we praise God in the midst of trials, our love shines through in a powerful way. Worship not only transforms the atmosphere around us, but it also changes our hearts.

Closing Prayer:

Father, I choose to worship You with all my heart. Let my praise be sincere and my worship be pleasing to You. Teach me to honor You not just with my lips but with my life. In Jesus' name, Amen.

Prayer Points:

- Lord, fill my heart with a spirit of worship that is not dependent on circumstances.

- Father, let my praise be an offering of love that honors You daily.

- Holy Spirit, teach me to worship God in spirit and in truth.

Day 12

DWELLING IN HIS HOUSE

Scripture:

Psalm 84:10 – *"Better is one day in Your courts than a thousand elsewhere; I would rather be a doorkeeper in the house of my God than dwell in the tents of the wicked."*

Psalm 122:1 – *"I was glad when they said to me, 'Let us go into the house of the LORD.'"*

Reflection:

To love God is to love His house. There's something special about being in the presence of God with His people. Dwelling in His house isn't just about attending services; it's about craving fellowship with God and His family.

Family reunions often bring warmth and joy, with relatives traveling from afar just to sit together, laugh, and reconnect. God designed His house to be that kind of place: a gathering where His people are refreshed, strengthened, and reminded that we belong to Him and to one another.

David expressed this longing when he wrote, *"One*

thing I ask of the LORD... that I may dwell in the house of the LORD all the days of my life" (Psalm 27:4). His passion for God's house reflected his deep love for God.

In a world full of distractions, choosing to dwell in God's house helps us stay aligned with Him. When we gather, we uplift one another, grow together, and experience His presence in meaningful ways. Loving God means valuing the privilege of worship, fellowship, and service in His house.

Closing Prayer:

Lord, I love Your house and the place where Your glory dwells. Let my heart always be drawn to Your presence and to fellowship with Your people. In Jesus' name, Amen.

Prayer Points:

- Father, increase my hunger for Your presence and my love for Your house.
- Lord, let every time I gather in Your house bring transformation and growth.
- Holy Spirit, help me to serve faithfully in the house of God with joy.

Day 13

OBEDIENCE AS THE GREATEST EXPRESSION OF LOVE

Scripture:

John 14:15 – *"If you love Me, keep My commandments."*

1 John 5:3 – *"In fact, this is love for God: to keep His commands. And His commands are not burdensome."*

Reflection:

The truest proof of love for God is our obedience. While expressing affection is important, it's our actions that demonstrate the authenticity of that love.

We might say "I love you," but it's our actions that truly show it. A child who listens to a parent's guidance expresses love more clearly than one who disregards it. Similarly, God recognizes the depth of our love not just through our words, but through our willingness to follow His commandments.

Abraham serves as a powerful example of this. When God asked him to sacrifice Isaac, the son he had long awaited, Abraham obeyed without hesitation (Genesis 22). His willingness to obey reflected his profound love and trust in God, leading to blessings beyond measure.

At times, obedience may require us to make sacrifices, surrender our desires, or step outside our comfort zones. Yet, it's through our obedience that we truly show our devotion. Love is not just a feeling; it's a choice we make through our actions.

Closing Prayer:

Father, help me to love You through obedience. Give me a willing heart that delights in doing Your will, even when it is difficult. In Jesus' name, Amen.

Prayer Points:

1. Lord, give me the grace to obey You in every area of my life.

2. Father, remove every spirit of rebellion or disobedience from my heart.

3. Holy Spirit, empower me to walk in daily obedience as an expression of love for God.

Day 14

GUARDING OUR LOVE AGAINST WORLDLINESS

Scripture:

1 John 2:15–17 – *"Do not love the world or anything in the world. If anyone loves the world, love for the Father is not in them. For everything in the world — the lust of the flesh, the lust of the eyes, and the pride of life — comes not from the Father but from the world. The world and its desires pass away, but whoever does the will of God lives forever."*

Reflection:

Love for God is something we must cherish and protect. The biggest challenge to our love for Him is worldliness — living as if this life is all there is.

Think of a bride who is engaged to be married; she guards her devotion, not letting distractions pull her heart away from her beloved. That's how the church, as Christ's bride, is called to live. Our love for Him must be safeguarded, because when our affections are divided, our devotion weakens and we risk losing our joy.

Take Demas, for example. He was once a close companion of Paul but chose to abandon his calling because he "loved this present world" (2 Timothy 4:10). His story serves as a warning that divided love can lead to spiritual decline. In contrast, those who prioritize their love for God over worldly desires remain strong and fruitful. We must choose whom we will love – God or other things. We cannot love both equally.

Protecting our love requires daily decisions — choosing prayer over compromise, purity over fleeting pleasure, and embracing God's truth rather than the lies of culture. It's a challenging path, but with the support of the Holy Spirit, it is entirely possible.

Closing Prayer:

Lord, guard my heart from the love of the world. Help me to keep my devotion pure and my affection set on You alone. In Jesus' name, Amen.

Prayer Points:

- Father, deliver me from every worldly desire that competes with my love for You.

- Lord, help me to value eternal treasures more than temporary pleasures.

- Holy Spirit, strengthen me to stand firm in my love for God until the end.

Day 15

LOVING OTHERS AS OURSELVES

Scripture:

Matthew 22:39 – *"And the second is like it: 'Love your neighbor as yourself.'"*

1 John 4:20 – *"Whoever claims to love God yet hates a brother or sister is a liar. For whoever does not love their brother and sister, whom they have seen, cannot love God, whom they have not seen."*

Reflection:

One of the clearest ways to show our love for God is by loving those around us. Jesus connected the two — our love for God and our love for people. The way we treat others reveals how deeply we are devoted to Him.

On the road to Jericho, the priest and Levite looked away from a man in need, but the Samaritan stopped, knelt down, and offered his help. His compassion spoke louder than any title or position. Loving others is never about convenience; it's about making our love for God visible through our actions.

In our modern world, "neighbors" are not just the people who live next door but anyone God places in our lives — coworkers, classmates, family members, or even strangers. Loving others doesn't always require grand gestures; sometimes it can be as simple as listening, forgiving, or showing a little kindness.

When we love others as ourselves, we reflect God's heart. Love that we keep to ourselves feels incomplete, but love that we share becomes a testament to God's presence within us.

Closing Prayer:

Father, teach me to love people as You have loved me. Remove pride, selfishness, and bitterness from my heart. Let my life reflect Your love in action. In Jesus' name, Amen.

Prayer Points:

- Lord, give me compassion to see others the way You see them.
- Father, help me to love even those who are difficult to love.
- Holy Spirit, let my daily actions reveal God's love to my family, friends, and community.

Day 16

ENCOURAGING OUR HOUSEHOLD TO LOVE THE LORD

Scripture:
Joshua 24:15 – *"But as for me and my household, we will serve the LORD."*

Deuteronomy 6:6–7 – *"These commandments that I give you today are to be on your hearts. Impress them on your children. Talk about them when you sit at home and when you walk along the road, when you lie down and when you get up."*

Reflection:

Love for God should not stop with us — it should overflow into our homes. True discipleship begins in the family. Joshua understood this when he boldly declared, "As for me and my house, we will serve the LORD."

Around the dinner table, families share stories, laughter, and lessons that shape their identities. Faith is passed along in much the same way — not just through instruction, but through daily example. A praying parent, a Scripture read together, or a gentle word of encouragement plants seeds that grow into lasting devotion.

Timothy's faith was shaped by his mother Eunice and grandmother Lois (2 Timothy 1:5). Their love for God impacted him so deeply that he became a significant leader in the early church. This reminds us that everyday faithfulness at home can raise generations of people who love and serve the Lord.

Encouraging your household is not about forcing religion but modeling love. When children, spouses, or relatives see sincerity in your devotion, they are drawn to follow your example.

Closing Prayer:

Lord, let my home be a dwelling place of Your presence. Help me to lead by example and inspire my family to love and serve You faithfully. In Jesus' name, Amen.

Prayer Points:

- Father, make my household a family that loves and serves You wholeheartedly.
- Lord, help me to be a living example of devotion that inspires my family.
- Holy Spirit, raise generations after me who will carry the flame of love for God.

Day 17

GENEROUS AND SACRIFICIAL GIVING

Scripture:

2 Corinthians 8:3–4 – *"For I testify that they gave as much as they were able, and even beyond their ability. Entirely on their own, they urgently pleaded with us for the privilege of sharing in this service to the Lord's people."*

Mark 12:43–44 – *"Truly I tell you, this poor widow has put more into the treasury than all the others. They all gave out of their wealth; but she, out of her poverty, put in everything — all she had to live on."*

Reflection:

Love is not just something we say; it's something we show through our actions. One of the most powerful ways to express our love for God is through generosity. When we give selflessly to support His work and help those in need, we demonstrate that our hearts are not tied to our possessions but are grounded in Him.

In Macedonia, believers who faced poverty still found joy in giving, regardless of their circumstances. Their willingness to share was a testament to their open hearts. Similarly, a poor widow in the temple contributed two small coins, and Jesus highlighted her gift as the most significant because it represented true sacrifice. Love shines brightest when it reaches beyond our comfort zones.

Those two coins represented her trust, her surrender, and her love for God. What others saw as little, Jesus recognized as everything. Her offering revealed a heart fully devoted to God, proving that true delight is measured not by amount, but by devotion.

Loving God through our giving isn't about how much we give, but about the sacrifice we make in the process. When we dedicate our time, resources, and even our comfort to advance God's kingdom, we mirror His love, for He gave us His very best—His Son.

Closing Prayer:

Lord, thank You for being the ultimate Giver. Help me to give generously and joyfully, not out of compulsion but out of love for You. In Jesus' name, Amen.

Prayer Points:

- Father, give me a heart of generosity that reflects Your love.
- Lord, help me to see giving as an opportunity to honor You, not a burden.

- Holy Spirit, teach me to give sacrificially and cheerfully for the advancement of God's kingdom.

Day 18

FEEDING HIS SHEEP

Scripture:

John 21:17 – *"The third time He said to him, 'Simon son of John, do you love Me?' Peter was hurt because Jesus asked him the third time, 'Do you love Me?' He said, 'Lord, You know all things; You know that I love You.' Jesus said, 'Feed My sheep.'"*

1 Peter 5:2 – *"Be shepherds of God's flock that is under your care, watching over them — not because you must, but because you are willing, as God wants you to be; not pursuing dishonest gain, but eager to serve."*

Reflection:

Loving God goes beyond just personal devotion; it involves caring for others spiritually. When Jesus asked Peter if he loved Him, He didn't say, "sing louder" or "pray longer." Instead, He said, "feed My sheep." Our love for God is demonstrated in how we nurture His people.

Parents understand the daily challenge of feeding a child—sometimes messy, sometimes inconvenient, but always essential. This imagery reflects Jesus' command to Peter: "If you love Me, feed My sheep."

Caring for others spiritually, whether through prayer, encouragement, or teaching, is a profound way to express our love for God that words alone cannot capture.

Feeding God's sheep isn't just the responsibility of pastors; it's a calling for every believer. It can be as simple as sharing a Bible verse with a friend, praying for a coworker, or mentoring a younger believer in their journey with Christ. Every act of spiritual care is a heartfelt way of saying, "Lord, I love You."

Jesus linked Peter's love for Him with his willingness to care for others. If we genuinely love God, we cannot overlook the spiritual needs of those around us.

Closing Prayer:

Father, help me to demonstrate my love for You by caring for the people around me. Show me how to feed Your sheep with encouragement, prayer, and truth. In Jesus' name, Amen.

Prayer Points:

- Lord, give me a shepherd's heart to care for those You place in my path.
- Father, use me to encourage and strengthen the faith of others.
- Holy Spirit, empower me to feed God's sheep with wisdom, love, and truth.

Day 19

PASSION FOR SOULS AND EVANGELISM

Scripture:

Matthew 28:19–20 — *"Therefore go and make disciples of all nations, baptizing them in the name of the Father and of the Son and of the Holy Spirit, and teaching them to obey everything I have commanded you. And surely I am with you always, to the very end of the age."*

Romans 10:14 — *"How, then, can they call on the one they have not believed in? And how can they believe in the one of whom they have not heard? And how can they hear without someone preaching to them?"*

Reflection:

One of the greatest expressions of love for God is a passion for souls. When we truly love God, we naturally love what He loves — and nothing matters more to Him than people.

When someone discovers a cure that saves lives, they don't keep it to themselves; they share it with urgency. The gospel is far greater, and silence is simply not an option. Our love for God compels us to speak out, because what matters most to Him is rescuing people from darkness.

The early disciples showed us this truth. Even in the face of persecution, they couldn't stop preaching about Jesus. Their passion for souls stemmed from their love for the Lord who had saved them. Paul wrote, "The love of Christ compels us" (2 Corinthians 5:14). It was their love for God that drove them to reach others.

Evangelism isn't just for pastors or missionaries; it's the calling of every believer. It can be as simple as inviting a neighbor to church, sharing your personal story with a friend, or showing kindness that opens the door for the gospel. When we have a passion for souls, we reflect the heart of the God who leaves the ninety-nine to rescue the one.

Closing Prayer:

Lord, give me Your heart for the lost. Let my love for You overflow into a passion for souls. Use me to share Your truth and draw others into Your kingdom. In Jesus' name, Amen.

Prayer Points:

1. Father, fill me with compassion for the lost and the boldness to reach them.

2. Lord, open doors of opportunity for me to share Your love with others.

3. Holy Spirit, empower me to be an effective witness of Jesus in my generation.

Day 20

ZEAL FOR GOD'S HOUSE

Scripture:

Psalm 69:9 – *"For zeal for Your house consumes me, and the insults of those who insult You fall on me."*

John 2:17 – *"His disciples remembered that it is written: 'Zeal for Your house will consume me.'"*

Reflection:

When we truly love God, we develop a genuine passion for His house. Having zeal for God's house means caring deeply about His presence, His worship, and His people.

When Jesus walked into the temple and found it turned into a marketplace, His passion surged as He restored it to a house of prayer. Zeal for God's house looks like that: not just casual attendance, but a heartfelt commitment to His presence, His people, and the place where His name is honored.

Think about someone renovating their home. They invest time, money, and energy to make it beautiful because they truly care about it. Loving God's house means we treat it with that same passion — showing up faithfully, serving joyfully, giving generously, and praying earnestly for the church to thrive.

David captured this sentiment when he said, "I was glad when they said to me, 'Let us go into the house of the Lord'" (Psalm 122:1). For him, God's house was not a burden but a source of joy.

When we are zealous for God's house, we attend and actively invest in it. We pray for it, serve in it, and protect its unity. Our passion for God is reflected in our passion for His house. We also demonstrate love by ensuring the house of God is cared for physically.

Closing Prayer:

Father, give me zeal for Your house. Let me love and honor Your church with joy, faithfulness, and service. May my devotion strengthen Your work on earth. In Jesus' name, Amen.

Prayer Points:

- Lord, fill me with passion for Your house and the work of Your kingdom.
- Father, help me to serve faithfully and joyfully in my local church.
- Holy Spirit, use me as a vessel to strengthen, build, and protect God's house.

Day 21

LOVING GOD IN THE MIDST OF TRIALS

Scripture:

Job 13:15 – *"Though He slay me, yet will I hope in Him; I will surely defend my ways to His face."*

Romans 8:35 – *"Who shall separate us from the love of Christ? Shall trouble or hardship or persecution or famine or nakedness or danger or sword?"*

Reflection:

True love for God is truly proven not in easy times but in trials. Anyone can sing when the sun is shining, but it takes a deep, abiding love to keep praising God in the storms of life.

Job stands as a timeless example. He lost his children, wealth, health, and reputation, yet he refused to curse God. Instead, he declared, "Though He slay me, yet will I hope in Him" (Job 13:15). His love for God was rooted not in blessings but in genuine devotion.

Though Job lacked full understanding, he remained steadfast in love and trust toward God.

Wedding vows promise love "for better or worse, in sickness and in health." Real devotion is tested in hardship. Job embodied this kind of love for God — stripped of health, wealth, and family, yet boldly declaring, "Though He slay me, yet will I trust Him." Trials reveal whether our love is based on circumstances or if it is steadfast.

Paul echoed this sentiment when he wrote that nothing — not hardship, persecution, or even death — could separate us from the love of Christ. When our love for God remains strong in trials, we show the world that He is worthy of our devotion, no matter the circumstances.

Closing Prayer:

Father, give me a steadfast heart that loves You in every season. Strengthen me to remain faithful in trials, trusting that You are always with me. In Jesus' name, Amen.

Prayer Points:

- Lord, help me to love You even when life is difficult or confusing.

- Father, turn my trials into testimonies that glorify Your name.

- Holy Spirit, fill me with endurance and faith to keep loving God in every circumstance.

Day 22

INTIMACY WITH GOD

Scripture:

Deuteronomy 30:20 – *"And that you may love the LORD your God, listen to His voice, and hold fast to Him. For the LORD is your life, and He will give you many years in the land He swore to give to your fathers, Abraham, Isaac, and Jacob."*

Psalm 63:1 – *"O God, You are my God; early will I seek You; my soul thirsts for You; my flesh longs for You in a dry and thirsty land where there is no water."*

Reflection:

At the heart of loving God is intimacy — a close, personal relationship where you truly get to know Him and walk with Him every day. Intimacy goes beyond just routine prayers or attending church; it's about forming a heartfelt connection with your Creator.

David craved this kind of closeness. In Psalm 63, he described a longing for God that transcended mere religious practices. He likened his thirst for God to a man in a desert desperately needing water. That's what intimacy is all about — a profound desire for His presence.

Close friendships rely on more than just small talk. Sharing secrets, laughter, and even tears strengthens the bond. That's what intimacy with God feels like — not a distant relationship but a deep connection where we share our lives with Him and draw near to His presence every day.

When we seek intimacy with God, He becomes our greatest joy, our safest haven, and our closest friend. We begin to serve Him not out of obligation, but out of deep love and trust. Intimacy transforms our relationship with Him from a mere religion into a genuine connection.

Closing Prayer:

Lord, draw me closer to You every day. Remove every barrier that keeps me from intimacy with You. Let my love for You grow deeper as I walk in Your presence. In Jesus' name, Amen.

Prayer Points:

1. Father, increase my hunger and thirst for Your presence daily.

2. Lord, help me to build a consistent lifestyle of prayer and fellowship with You.

3. Holy Spirit, reveal more of God's heart to me as I walk in intimacy with Him.

Day 23

ACCESS TO GOD'S BEST

Scripture:

1 Corinthians 2:9 – *"However, as it is written: 'What no eye has seen, what no ear has heard, and what no human mind has conceived' — the things God has prepared for those who love Him."*

Psalm 84:11 – *"For the LORD God is a sun and shield; the LORD bestows favor and honor; no good thing does He withhold from those whose walk is blameless."*

Reflection:

Loving God opens the door to His very best. The world offers temporary pleasures, but God's love unlocks blessings, favor, and treasures that go far beyond what we can imagine.

Parents sometimes save a special gift for the right moment, waiting until their child is ready to truly appreciate it. God does the same. His greatest blessings are reserved for those who love Him—treasures beyond what our eyes have seen or our ears have heard—given at just the right time.

Abraham's life is a powerful testimony to this truth.

Because he loved and obeyed God, he experienced blessings so immense that entire nations were born through him. His life reminds us that God's best is not always immediate, but it is always worth the wait. At this time, God is forming our character to sustain the blessing. Both spiritual and natural maturity are required. A child crowned as king would devastate a nation; preparation is mercy.

When we love God sincerely, we gain access to His wisdom, favor, and guidance. We may not always understand His timing, but His best always exceeds our expectations. Loving Him aligns us with a future full of hope.

Closing Prayer:

Father, thank You for preparing Your best for me. Teach me to trust Your timing and to walk in love so I may experience all that You have promised. In Jesus' name, Amen.

Prayer Points:

- Lord, align my desires with Your perfect will so I may walk in Your best.

- Father, remove every distraction that keeps me from receiving what You've prepared.

- Holy Spirit, help me to wait patiently and faithfully for God's promises to unfold.

Day 24

COVENANT BLESSINGS FOR THOSE WHO LOVE HIM

Scripture:

Deuteronomy 7:9 – *"Know therefore that the LORD your God is God; He is the faithful God, keeping His covenant of love to a thousand generations of those who love Him and keep His commandments."*

Nehemiah 1:5 – *"Lord, the God of heaven, the great and awesome God, who keeps His covenant of love with those who love Him and keep His commandments."*

Reflection:

God's love isn't just a casual feeling; it's a deep, binding promise known as a covenant. A covenant signifies a powerful commitment that cannot be broken. When we love Him and choose to follow His ways, we enter into a relationship that brings blessings not just for ourselves, but for our future generations as well.

Think of a father who carefully plans to leave an inheritance for his children and grandchildren, ensuring they are cared for long after he is gone. God's covenant works in much the same way. His promises extend beyond our own lives, reaching those who walk in love and obedience to Him for years to come.

Take David, for example. Because of his love and devotion to God, mercy and favor were shown to his descendants, even when they stumbled. The blessings of the covenant lasted well beyond his time. Your love for God today can have a profound impact on your children, grandchildren, and even further down the line.

God is always faithful to uphold His promises. When we choose love and obedience, we not only secure blessings for ourselves but also create a spiritual legacy that holds eternal significance.

Closing Prayer:

Lord, thank You for being a covenant-keeping God. Help me to walk faithfully in Your love so that generations after me will experience Your blessings. In Jesus' name, Amen.

Prayer Points:

- Father, let my love for You establish a covenant of blessings over my family line.
- Lord, help me to live in obedience so I can walk fully in Your promises.
- Holy Spirit, strengthen me to leave a godly legacy for future generations.

Day 25

FAITHFULNESS AND DIVINE ACKNOWLEDGMENT

Scripture:

Numbers 12:7 – *"But this is not true of My servant Moses; he is faithful in all My house."*

Hebrews 3:5–6 – *"Moses was faithful as a servant in all God's house... But Christ is faithful as the Son over God's house. And we are His house, if indeed we hold firmly to our confidence and the hope in which we glory."*

Reflection:

Loving God nurtures a deep sense of faithfulness. To be faithful means being consistent, reliable, and unwavering in our devotion. When we demonstrate our faithfulness to God, He acknowledges us before both heaven and earth.

Moses exemplifies this beautifully. Despite his imperfections, he remained a dedicated servant in God's house. His love for the Lord gave him the strength to lead Israel through the wilderness. God Himself praised Moses' faithfulness. What greater recognition could one hope for?

An employee who dedicates years of hard work may not be noticed by everyone, but the owner sees their commitment and eventually rewards their loyalty. In the same way, God recognized Moses' faithfulness and commended him personally. Our love for God fosters this kind of steadfastness — a devotion that endures even when no one else is cheering for us.

When we love God, we stay committed in our devotion, regardless of applause, challenges, or the cost of obedience. In due time, God honors that faithfulness.

Closing Prayer:

Lord, help me to be faithful in all things — in prayer, service, and obedience. Let my love for You be steadfast, and may my life bring You glory. In Jesus' name, Amen.

Prayer Points:

- Father, strengthen me to remain faithful in every season of life.

- Lord, let my love for You be evident through consistent obedience.

- Holy Spirit, help me to live in such a way that God Himself acknowledges my faithfulness.

Day 26

ALL THINGS WORK TOGETHER FOR LOVERS OF GOD

Scripture:

Romans 8:28 – *"And we know that in all things God works for the good of those who love Him, who have been called according to His purpose."*

Genesis 50:20 – *"You intended to harm me, but God intended it for good to accomplish what is now being done, the saving of many lives."*

Reflection:

One of the greatest comforts for those who love God is the assurance that He works everything—yes, even the painful and confusing moments of life—for our ultimate good.

Take Joseph's story, for example. After being betrayed by his brothers, sold into slavery, and unjustly imprisoned, his life seemed completely shattered. Yet, in the end, Joseph could confidently say, *"You intended to harm me, but God intended it for good."* His unwavering love and faith in God turned his trials into triumphs.

A master weaver at a loom, pulling threads that, up close, look tangled and messy. But when the work is done, the design is breathtaking. Life often feels like those loose threads, but God skillfully weaves them into a beautiful masterpiece. For those who love Him, even the hardest seasons can be shaped into something good.

This truth doesn't suggest that everything that happens is good, but it does mean that God can bring good out of every situation for those who love Him. Also, remember that all things work together for good because God has already gone ahead of us.

Closing Prayer:
Father, thank You for working all things together for my good. Teach me to trust You when life doesn't make sense, knowing that Your plan is perfect. In Jesus' name, Amen.

Prayer Points:

- Lord, help me to trust You even when circumstances look unfavorable.
- Father, turn every trial in my life into a testimony of Your goodness.
- Holy Spirit, remind me daily that God is weaving all things together for my good.

Day 27

DIVINE RESCUE AND PROTECTION

Scripture:

Psalm 91:14–15 – *"Because he loves Me," says the LORD, "I will rescue him; I will protect him, for he acknowledges My name. He will call on Me, and I will answer him; I will be with him in trouble, I will deliver him and honor him."*

Isaiah 43:2 – *"When you pass through the waters, I will be with you; and when you pass through the rivers, they will not sweep over you. When you walk through the fire, you will not be burned; the flames will not set you ablaze."*

Reflection:

Loving God places us under the shelter of His protection. He doesn't guarantee a life free from challenges, but He does assure us of His presence, rescue, and safety amid them.

Imagine a child gripping their father's hand tightly while crossing a busy street, feeling secure despite the rush of traffic. That's a perfect illustration of God's protection. Our love for Him keeps us close to His hand, and His promise is unwavering: "Because he loves Me, I will rescue him."

Consider Daniel in the lions' den, the three Hebrew boys in the fiery furnace, and Paul during shipwrecks; they all bear witness to this truth. Their love and loyalty to God didn't shield them from trials, but it did ensure divine rescue in the face of danger.

God's promise is personal: *"Because he loves Me, I will rescue him."* Love opens the door to divine protection. In Christ, we are never alone — and we are never without His saving power.

Closing Prayer:

Lord, thank You for being my protector and deliverer. Keep me under the shadow of Your wings, and let my love for You draw me deeper into Your safety. In Jesus' name, Amen.

Prayer Points:

- Father, surround me and my family with Your hedge of divine protection.

- Lord, deliver me from every trap and danger designed by the enemy.

- Holy Spirit, strengthen my faith to trust God's rescue in every circumstance.

Day 28

PEACE AND CONTENTMENT

Scripture:

Isaiah 26:3 – *"You will keep in perfect peace those whose minds are steadfast, because they trust in You."*

Philippians 4:11 – *"I have learned to be content whatever the circumstances."*

Reflection:

Loving God brings a deep sense of peace that remains steady, no matter what life throws our way. While the world might suggest that comfort comes from our possessions or achievements, it is only through God that we can find true peace and lasting contentment.

Paul discovered this truth firsthand. He went through times of both plenty and struggle, yet he wrote, *"I have learned to be content whatever the circumstances."* His sense of contentment didn't depend on what was happening around him but was firmly rooted in his relationship with Christ.

A baby resting in a mother's arms, completely at ease, not worrying about what tomorrow holds — that love provides a sense of safety. Similarly, those who truly love God experience a peace that transcends their circumstances and a contentment that isn't tied to material things. Trust serves as an anchor for the heart, keeping fear at bay.

This peace doesn't deny the reality of life's challenges; instead, it grounds us in God's unwavering faithfulness. It teaches us that true satisfaction isn't found in what we possess but in our connection to Him. Loving God shifts our focus from the endless pursuit of more to a restful trust in Him.

Closing Prayer:

Father, thank You for the peace that comes from loving You. Teach me contentment in every season, and let my heart rest in Your faithfulness. In Jesus' name, Amen.

Prayer Points:

- Lord, guard my heart with Your peace in every situation.
- Father, help me to be content in You and not chase after temporary satisfaction.
- Holy Spirit, keep my mind stayed on God so I may walk in perfect peace.

Day 29

TRANSFORMATION AND SPIRITUAL GROWTH

Scripture:

2 Corinthians 3:18 – *"And we all, who with unveiled faces contemplate the Lord's glory, are being transformed into His image with ever-increasing glory, which comes from the Lord, who is the Spirit."*

Galatians 5:22–23 – *"But the fruit of the Spirit is love, joy, peace, forbearance, kindness, goodness, faithfulness, gentleness and self-control."*

Reflection:

Loving God doesn't leave us unchanged, it transforms us. When we focus our attention on Him, His Spirit works within us, shaping our character to reflect Christ.

Clay in a potter's hands starts off as ordinary, formless, and rough. But with careful pressure and shaping, it becomes a beautiful vessel with purpose. Our love for God works in much the same way. As we surrender to Him, His Spirit gradually transforms us into the image of Christ each day.

This transformation is not instantaneous but progressive. As we walk with God day by day, our hearts soften, our minds are renewed, and our actions align more closely with His will. The more we love Him, the more His fruits – love, patience, kindness, and self-control, become evident in our lives.

Loving God is not just about words or feelings; it's about becoming more like Him. True love grows, and as it grows, it changes us.

Closing Prayer:

Lord, I yield myself to Your transforming power. Let my love for You produce spiritual growth and fruit that glorifies Your name. In Jesus' name, Amen.

Prayer Points:

- Father, change me daily into the image of Christ as I walk in Your love.
- Lord, let my life bear the fruit of the Spirit for all to see.
- Holy Spirit, remove anything in me that hinders transformation and growth.

Day 30

PURPOSE AND FULFILLMENT

Scripture:

Psalm 37:4 – *"Take delight in the LORD, and He will give you the desires of your heart."*

Ephesians 2:10 – *"For we are God's handiwork, created in Christ Jesus to do good works, which God prepared in advance for us to do."*

Reflection:

Loving God helps us find our true purpose. Each of us has been created with a unique assignment, and it's through our love for Him that we uncover what makes life fulfilling.

Think of a key; it may seem small and unimportant until it fits into the lock it was made for. Only then does it reveal its true purpose. Our lives are similar, we find fulfillment when we align ourselves with God's will. Loving Him unlocks the destiny we were meant to embrace.

David discovered fulfillment not in his rise to kingship, but in serving God's purposes during his time (Acts 13:36). Paul found joy in dedicating his life to spreading the gospel. True fulfillment doesn't come from pursuing personal achievements but from cherishing God and fulfilling the unique role He designed for us.

When you prioritize your love for God, He places His desires in your heart and guides you to act on them. Purpose without God feels hollow, but with Him, it becomes vibrant and everlasting.

Closing Prayer:

Father, thank You for creating me with purpose. As I love You, reveal Your plans for my life and help me walk in them with joy and fulfillment. In Jesus' name, Amen.

Prayer Points:

- Lord, let my love for You align me with the purpose You created me for.
- Father, reveal the assignments You've prepared for me to fulfill in this season.
- Holy Spirit, guide me to live a life of impact and eternal significance.

Day 31

LOVING GOD – THE KEY TO ETERNAL LIFE

Scripture:

Luke 10:27–28 – *"He answered, 'Love the Lord your God with all your heart and with all your soul and with all your strength and with all your mind'; and, 'Love your neighbor as yourself.' 'You have answered correctly,' Jesus replied. 'Do this and you will live.'"*

John 17:3 – *"Now this is eternal life: that they know You, the only true God, and Jesus Christ, whom You have sent."*

Reflection:

The ultimate reward for loving God is eternal life. Everything in this world eventually fades away, but those who love God will experience the joy of living forever in His presence.

When Jesus was asked about the greatest commandment, He emphasized the importance of loving both God and people, saying, *"Do this and you will live."* Loving God is not just the key to joy in this life; it also opens the door to eternal life with Him.

Consider a bride's years of waiting and preparing for her wedding day. When she finally unites with her groom, the joy she feels reflects the eternal union that awaits those who love God. While titles, possessions, and achievements may diminish, our love for Him ensures we have everlasting life in His presence.

At the end of our journey, what truly matters is not how much we accomplished but how deeply we loved Him. Eternal life is about knowing God, walking with Him, and living in His presence forever.

Closing Prayer:

Lord, thank You for the promise of eternal life through Jesus Christ. Keep my love for You strong until the very end, and prepare me for the joy of living with You forever. In Jesus' name, Amen.

Prayer Points:

- Father, keep my love for You steadfast until the day I see You face to face.

- Lord, prepare me daily for eternal life in Your presence.

- Holy Spirit, help me to live with eternity in view, loving God above all else.

ONE-YEAR BIBLE READING PLAN
(GENESIS TO REVELATION)

ONE-YEAR BIBLE READING PLAN
(GENESIS TO REVELATION)

Read through the entire Bible in one year — about 3–4 chapters per day. Includes a monthly memory verse for reflection and meditation.

Monthly Memory Verses

January:

Joshua 1:8 – 'This Book of the Law shall not depart from your mouth, but you shall meditate in it day and night...'

February:

1 Corinthians 13:13 – 'And now abide faith, hope, love, these three; but the greatest of these is love.'

March:

Philippians 4:13 – 'I can do all things through Christ who strengthens me.'

April:

Proverbs 3:5–6 – 'Trust in the Lord with all your heart, and lean not on your own understanding...'

May:

Isaiah 40:31 – 'But those who wait on the Lord shall renew their strength; they shall mount up with wings like eagles...'

June:

Romans 8:28 – 'And we know that all things work together for good to those who love God...'

July:

Psalm 23:1 – 'The Lord is my shepherd; I shall not want.'

August:

Ephesians 3:20 – 'Now to Him who is able to do exceedingly abundantly above all that we ask or think...'

September:

Galatians 6:9 – 'And let us not grow weary while doing good, for in due season we shall reap if we do not lose heart.'

October:

2 Timothy 1:7 – 'For God has not given us a spirit of fear, but of power and of love and of a sound mind.'

November:

Psalm 100:4 – 'Enter into His gates with thanksgiving, and into His courts with praise...'

December:

Luke 2:11 – 'For there is born to you this day in the city of David a Savior, who is Christ the Lord.'

WEEKLY READING PLAN

Week 1

- ○ Day 1: Genesis 1–3
- ○ Day 2: Genesis 4–7
- ○ Day 3: Genesis 8–11
- ○ Day 4: Genesis 12–15
- ○ Day 5: Genesis 16–18
- ○ Day 6: Genesis 19–21
- ○ Day 7: Genesis 22–24

Week 2

- ○ Day 8: Genesis 25–28
- ○ Day 9: Genesis 29–31
- ○ Day 10: Genesis 32–34
- ○ Day 11: Genesis 35–37
- ○ Day 12: Genesis 38–40
- ○ Day 13: Genesis 41–42
- ○ Day 14: Genesis 43–45

Week 3

- ○ Day 15: Genesis 46–47
- ○ Day 16: Genesis 48–50
- ○ Day 17: Exodus 1–3
- ○ Day 18: Exodus 4–6
- ○ Day 19: Exodus 7–9
- ○ Day 20: Exodus 10–12
- ○ Day 21: Exodus 13–15

Week 4

- ◯ Day 22: Exodus 16–18
- ◯ Day 23: Exodus 19–21
- ◯ Day 24: Exodus 22–24
- ◯ Day 25: Exodus 25–27
- ◯ Day 26: Exodus 28–29
- ◯ Day 27: Exodus 30–32
- ◯ Day 28: Exodus 33–35

Week 5

- ◯ Day 29: Exodus 36–38
- ◯ Day 30: Exodus 39–40
- ◯ Day 31: Leviticus 1–4
- ◯ Day 32: Leviticus 5–7
- ◯ Day 33: Leviticus 8–10
- ◯ Day 34: Leviticus 11–13
- ◯ Day 35: Leviticus 14–15

Week 6

- ◯ Day 36: Leviticus 16–18
- ◯ Day 37: Leviticus 19–21
- ◯ Day 38: Leviticus 22–23
- ◯ Day 39: Leviticus 24–25
- ◯ Day 40: Leviticus 26–27
- ◯ Day 41: Numbers 1–2
- ◯ Day 42: Numbers 3–4

Week 7

- ◯ Day 43: Numbers 5–6
- ◯ Day 44: Numbers 7
- ◯ Day 45: Numbers 8–10
- ◯ Day 46: Numbers 11–13
- ◯ Day 47: Numbers 14–15
- ◯ Day 48: Numbers 16–17
- ◯ Day 49: Numbers 18–20

Week 8

- ◯ Day 50: Numbers 21–22
- ◯ Day 51: Numbers 23–25
- ◯ Day 52: Numbers 26–27
- ◯ Day 53: Numbers 28–30
- ◯ Day 54: Numbers 31–32
- ◯ Day 55: Numbers 33–34
- ◯ Day 56: Numbers 35–36

Week 9

- ◯ Day 57: Deuteronomy 1–2
- ◯ Day 58: Deuteronomy 3–4
- ◯ Day 59: Deuteronomy 5–7
- ◯ Day 60: Deuteronomy 8–10
- ◯ Day 61: Deuteronomy 11–13
- ◯ Day 62: Deuteronomy 14–16
- ◯ Day 63: Deuteronomy 17–20

Week 10

- ◯ Day 64: Deuteronomy 21–23
- ◯ Day 65: Deuteronomy 24–27
- ◯ Day 66: Deuteronomy 28–29
- ◯ Day 67: Deuteronomy 30–31
- ◯ Day 68: Deuteronomy 32–34
- ◯ Day 69: Joshua 1–3
- ◯ Day 70: Joshua 4–6

Week 11

- ◯ Day 71: Joshua 7–9
- ◯ Day 72: Joshua 10–12
- ◯ Day 73: Joshua 13–15
- ◯ Day 74: Joshua 16–18
- ◯ Day 75: Joshua 19–21
- ◯ Day 76: Joshua 22–24
- ◯ Day 77: Judges 1–3

Week 12

- ◯ Day 78: Judges 4–5
- ◯ Day 79: Judges 6–7
- ◯ Day 80: Judges 8–9
- ◯ Day 81: Judges 10–12
- ◯ Day 82: Judges 13–15
- ◯ Day 83: Judges 16–18
- ◯ Day 84: Judges 19–21

Week 13

- [ ] Day 85: Ruth 1–4
- [ ] Day 86: 1 Samuel 1–3
- [ ] Day 87: 1 Samuel 4–7
- [ ] Day 88: 1 Samuel 8–10
- [ ] Day 89: 1 Samuel 11–13
- [ ] Day 90: 1 Samuel 14–15
- [ ] Day 91: 1 Samuel 16–17

Week 14

- [ ] Day 92: 1 Samuel 18–20
- [ ] Day 93: 1 Samuel 21–24
- [ ] Day 94: 1 Samuel 25–27
- [ ] Day 95: 1 Samuel 28–31
- [ ] Day 96: 2 Samuel 1–3
- [ ] Day 97: 2 Samuel 4–7
- [ ] Day 98: 2 Samuel 8–10

Week 15

- [ ] Day 99: 2 Samuel 11–13
- [ ] Day 100: 2 Samuel 14–16
- [ ] Day 101: 2 Samuel 17–19
- [ ] Day 102: 2 Samuel 20–22
- [ ] Day 103: 2 Samuel 23–24
- [ ] Day 104: 1 Kings 1–2
- [ ] Day 105: 1 Kings 3–5

Week 16

- Day 106: 1 Kings 6–7
- Day 107: 1 Kings 8–9
- Day 108: 1 Kings 10–12
- Day 109: 1 Kings 13–15
- Day 110: 1 Kings 16–18
- Day 111: 1 Kings 19–20
- Day 112: 1 Kings 21–22

Week 17

- Day 113: 2 Kings 1–3
- Day 114: 2 Kings 4–5
- Day 115: 2 Kings 6–8
- Day 116: 2 Kings 9–11
- Day 117: 2 Kings 12–14
- Day 118: 2 Kings 15–17
- Day 119: 2 Kings 18–19

Week 18

- Day 120: 2 Kings 20–22
- Day 121: 2 Kings 23–25
- Day 122: 1 Chronicles 1–2
- Day 123: 1 Chronicles 3–5
- Day 124: 1 Chronicles 6–7
- Day 125: 1 Chronicles 8–10
- Day 126: 1 Chronicles 11–13

Week 19

- ◯ Day 127: 1 Chronicles 14–16
- ◯ Day 128: 1 Chronicles 17–19
- ◯ Day 129: 1 Chronicles 20–23
- ◯ Day 130: 1 Chronicles 24–26
- ◯ Day 131: 1 Chronicles 27–29
- ◯ Day 132: 2 Chronicles 1–4
- ◯ Day 133: 2 Chronicles 5–7

Week 20

- ◯ Day 134: 2 Chronicles 8–10
- ◯ Day 135: 2 Chronicles 11–14
- ◯ Day 136: 2 Chronicles 15–18
- ◯ Day 137: 2 Chronicles 19–21
- ◯ Day 138: 2 Chronicles 22–24
- ◯ Day 139: 2 Chronicles 25–27
- ◯ Day 140: 2 Chronicles 28–30

Week 21

- ◯ Day 141: 2 Chronicles 31–33
- ◯ Day 142: 2 Chronicles 34–36
- ◯ Day 143: Ezra 1–3
- ◯ Day 144: Ezra 4–6
- ◯ Day 145: Ezra 7–8
- ◯ Day 146: Ezra 9–10
- ◯ Day 147: Nehemiah 1–3

Week 22

- ◯ Day 148: Nehemiah 4–6
- ◯ Day 149: Nehemiah 7–9
- ◯ Day 150: Nehemiah 10–11
- ◯ Day 151: Nehemiah 12–13
- ◯ Day 152: Esther 1–3
- ◯ Day 153: Esther 4–7
- ◯ Day 154: Esther 8–10

Week 23

- ◯ Day 155: Job 1–3
- ◯ Day 156: Job 4–7
- ◯ Day 157: Job 8–10
- ◯ Day 158: Job 11–14
- ◯ Day 159: Job 15–17
- ◯ Day 160: Job 18–20
- ◯ Day 161: Job 21–23

Week 24

- ◯ Day 162: Job 24–28
- ◯ Day 163: Job 29–31
- ◯ Day 164: Job 32–34
- ◯ Day 165: Job 35–37
- ◯ Day 166: Job 38–39
- ◯ Day 167: Job 40–42
- ◯ Day 168: Psalm 1–4

Week 25

◯ Day 169: Psalm 5–8
◯ Day 170: Psalm 9–16
◯ Day 171: Psalm 17–20
◯ Day 172: Psalm 21–25
◯ Day 173: Psalm 26–31
◯ Day 174: Psalm 32–35
◯ Day 175: Psalm 36–39

Week 26

◯ Day 176: Psalm 40–45
◯ Day 177: Psalm 46–51
◯ Day 178: Psalm 52–59
◯ Day 179: Psalm 60–67
◯ Day 180: Psalm 68–71
◯ Day 181: Psalm 72–77
◯ Day 182: Psalm 78–79

Week 27

◯ Day 183: Psalm 80–85
◯ Day 184: Psalm 86–90
◯ Day 185: Psalm 91–97
◯ Day 186: Psalm 98–104
◯ Day 187: Psalm 105–107
◯ Day 188: Psalm 108–114
◯ Day 189: Psalm 115–118

Week 28

- ◯ Day 190: Psalm 119:1–88
- ◯ Day 191: Psalm 119:89–176
- ◯ Day 192: Psalm 120–131
- ◯ Day 193: Psalm 132–138
- ◯ Day 194: Psalm 139–143
- ◯ Day 195: Psalm 144–150
- ◯ Day 196: Proverbs 1–3

Week 29

- ◯ Day 197: Proverbs 4–7
- ◯ Day 198: Proverbs 8–11
- ◯ Day 199: Proverbs 12–15
- ◯ Day 200: Proverbs 16–19
- ◯ Day 201: Proverbs 20–22
- ◯ Day 202: Proverbs 23–26
- ◯ Day 203: Proverbs 27–31

Week 30

- ◯ Day 204: Ecclesiastes 1–4
- ◯ Day 205: Ecclesiastes 5–8
- ◯ Day 206: Ecclesiastes 9–12
- ◯ Day 207: Song of Solomon 1–4
- ◯ Day 208: Song of Solomon 5–8
- ◯ Day 209: Isaiah 1–4
- ◯ Day 210: Isaiah 5–8

Week 31

- ◯ Day 211: Isaiah 9–12
- ◯ Day 212: Isaiah 13–17
- ◯ Day 213: Isaiah 18–22
- ◯ Day 214: Isaiah 23–27
- ◯ Day 215: Isaiah 28–30
- ◯ Day 216: Isaiah 31–35
- ◯ Day 217: Isaiah 36–39

Week 32

- ◯ Day 218: Isaiah 40–43
- ◯ Day 219: Isaiah 44–47
- ◯ Day 220: Isaiah 48–51
- ◯ Day 221: Isaiah 52–55
- ◯ Day 222: Isaiah 56–59
- ◯ Day 223: Isaiah 60–63
- ◯ Day 224: Isaiah 64–66

Week 33

- ◯ Day 225: Jeremiah 1–3
- ◯ Day 226: Jeremiah 4–6
- ◯ Day 227: Jeremiah 7–9
- ◯ Day 228: Jeremiah 10–13
- ◯ Day 229: Jeremiah 14–17
- ◯ Day 230: Jeremiah 18–21
- ◯ Day 231: Jeremiah 22–24

Week 34

- ☐ Day 232: Jeremiah 25–27
- ☐ Day 233: Jeremiah 28–30
- ☐ Day 234: Jeremiah 31–33
- ☐ Day 235: Jeremiah 34–36
- ☐ Day 236: Jeremiah 37–39
- ☐ Day 237: Jeremiah 40–42
- ☐ Day 238: Jeremiah 43–45

Week 35

- ☐ Day 239: Jeremiah 46–48
- ☐ Day 240: Jeremiah 49–50
- ☐ Day 241: Jeremiah 51–52
- ☐ Day 242: Lamentations 1–2
- ☐ Day 243: Lamentations 3–5
- ☐ Day 244: Ezekiel 1–3
- ☐ Day 245: Ezekiel 4–7

Week 36

- ☐ Day 246: Ezekiel 8–11
- ☐ Day 247: Ezekiel 12–15
- ☐ Day 248: Ezekiel 16–18
- ☐ Day 249: Ezekiel 19–21
- ☐ Day 250: Ezekiel 22–24
- ☐ Day 251: Ezekiel 25–27
- ☐ Day 252: Ezekiel 28–30

Week 37

◯ Day 253: Ezekiel 31–33
◯ Day 254: Ezekiel 34–36
◯ Day 255: Ezekiel 37–39
◯ Day 256: Ezekiel 40–42
◯ Day 257: Ezekiel 43–45
◯ Day 258: Ezekiel 46–48
◯ Day 259: Daniel 1–3

Week 38

◯ Day 260: Daniel 4–6
◯ Day 261: Daniel 7–9
◯ Day 262: Daniel 10–12
◯ Day 263: Hosea 1–4
◯ Day 264: Hosea 5–9
◯ Day 265: Hosea 10–14
◯ Day 266: Joel 1–3

Week 39

◯ Day 267: Amos 1–3
◯ Day 268: Amos 4–6
◯ Day 269: Amos 7–9
◯ Day 270: Obadiah 1
◯ Day 271: Jonah 1–4
◯ Day 272: Micah 1–4
◯ Day 273: Micah 5–7

Week 40

- ◯ Day 274: Nahum 1–3
- ◯ Day 275: Habakkuk 1–3
- ◯ Day 276: Zephaniah 1–3
- ◯ Day 277: Haggai 1–2
- ◯ Day 278: Zechariah 1–3
- ◯ Day 279: Zechariah 4–6
- ◯ Day 280: Zechariah 7–9

Week 41

- ◯ Day 281: Zechariah 10–12
- ◯ Day 282: Zechariah 13–14
- ◯ Day 283: Malachi 1–4
- ◯ Day 284: Matthew 1–4
- ◯ Day 285: Matthew 5–7
- ◯ Day 286: Matthew 8–9
- ◯ Day 287: Matthew 10–12

Week 42

- ◯ Day 288: Matthew 13–14
- ◯ Day 289: Matthew 15–17
- ◯ Day 290: Matthew 18–20
- ◯ Day 291: Matthew 21–22
- ◯ Day 292: Matthew 23–24
- ◯ Day 293: Matthew 25–26
- ◯ Day 294: Matthew 27–28

Week 43

- ○ Day 295: Mark 1–3
- ○ Day 296: Mark 4–5
- ○ Day 297: Mark 6–7
- ○ Day 298: Mark 8–9
- ○ Day 299: Mark 10–11
- ○ Day 300: Mark 12–13
- ○ Day 301: Mark 14–16

Week 44

- ○ Day 302: Luke 1–2
- ○ Day 303: Luke 3–4
- ○ Day 304: Luke 5–6
- ○ Day 305: Luke 7–8
- ○ Day 306: Luke 9–10
- ○ Day 307: Luke 11–12
- ○ Day 308: Luke 13–15

Week 45

- ○ Day 309: Luke 16–17
- ○ Day 310: Luke 18–19
- ○ Day 311: Luke 20–21
- ○ Day 312: Luke 22–24
- ○ Day 313: John 1–3
- ○ Day 314: John 4–5
- ○ Day 315: John 6–8

Week 46

- ◯ Day 316: John 9–11
- ◯ Day 317: John 12–14
- ◯ Day 318: John 15–17
- ◯ Day 319: John 18–19
- ◯ Day 320: John 20–21
- ◯ Day 321: Acts 1–3
- ◯ Day 322: Acts 4–6

Week 47

- ◯ Day 323: Acts 7–9
- ◯ Day 324: Acts 10–12
- ◯ Day 325: Acts 13–14
- ◯ Day 326: Acts 15–16
- ◯ Day 327: Acts 17–19
- ◯ Day 328: Acts 20–22
- ◯ Day 329: Acts 23–25

Week 48

- ◯ Day 330: Acts 26–28
- ◯ Day 331: Romans 1–3
- ◯ Day 332: Romans 4–7
- ◯ Day 333: Romans 8–10
- ◯ Day 334: Romans 11–13
- ◯ Day 335: Romans 14–16
- ◯ Day 336: 1 Corinthians 1–4

Week 49

- ◯ Day 337: 1 Corinthians 5–9
- ◯ Day 338: 1 Corinthians 10–13
- ◯ Day 339: 1 Corinthians 14–16
- ◯ Day 340: 2 Corinthians 1–4
- ◯ Day 341: 2 Corinthians 5–9
- ◯ Day 342: 2 Corinthians 10–13
- ◯ Day 343: Galatians 1–3

Week 50

- ◯ Day 344: Galatians 4–6
- ◯ Day 345: Ephesians 1–3
- ◯ Day 346: Ephesians 4–6
- ◯ Day 347: Philippians 1–4
- ◯ Day 348: Colossians 1–4
- ◯ Day 349: 1 Thessalonians 1–5
- ◯ Day 350: 2 Thessalonians 1–3

Week 51

- ◯ Day 351: 1 Timothy 1–6
- ◯ Day 352: 2 Timothy 1–4
- ◯ Day 353: Titus 1–3
- ◯ Day 354: Philemon 1
- ◯ Day 355: Hebrews 1–4
- ◯ Day 356: Hebrews 5–8
- ◯ Day 357: Hebrews 9–13

Week 52

- ○ Day 358: James 1–5
- ○ Day 359: 1 Peter 1–5
- ○ Day 360: 2 Peter 1–3
- ○ Day 361: 1 John 1–5
- ○ Day 362: 2 John, 3 John, Jude
- ○ Day 363: Revelation 1–3
- ○ Day 364: Revelation 4–8

Week 53

- ○ Day 365: Revelation 9–12
- ○ Day 366: Revelation 13–16
- ○ Day 367: Revelation 17–19
- ○ Day 368: Revelation 20–22

NOTES

NOTES

NOTES

NOTES

Notes

NOTES

NOTES

www.ingramcontent.com/pod-product-compliance
Lightning Source LLC
Chambersburg PA
CBHW070650050426
42451CB00008B/329